Cantonese for Kids: A Cantonese-English Book

Goh Goh and Dai Dai's BIG DAY WITH ELEPHANT

哥哥弟弟和大笨象好開心的一天

by K Yee

art by Tanja Russita

For a free audio recording and other books visit:
www.greencowsbooks.com

Goh Goh, the **stuff** is everywhere!

哥 哥 ， 啲 嘢 邊 度 都 係 ！

go4 go1 di1 je5 bin1 dou6 dou1 hai6

goh goh dee yeh bean doh doh high

Dai Dai, who made it so **messy**?

弟 弟 ， 邊 個 攪 到 咁 撈 攪 呀 ？

dai6 dai6 bin1 go3 gaau2 dou3 gam3 laau2 gaau6 aa3

dai dai bean guo gow doh gum lau gow ah

哥哥 Older Brother
go4 go1 (*goh goh*)

弟弟 Younger Brother
dai6 dai6 (*dai dai*)

氣球 Balloon
hei3 kau4 (*hay kuw*)

恤衫 Shirt
seot1 saam1 (*soot sahm*)

手套 Gloves
sau2 tou3 (*suw toe*)

奶嘴 Pacifier
naai5 zeoi2 (*nye jeoi*)

褸 Jacket
lau1 (*luw*)

襪 Socks
mat6 (*mutt*)

褲 Pants
fu3 (*foo*)

It's **Elephant**! He's in the **living room**!

係	大	笨	象	！	佢	喺	客	廳	！
hai6	daai6	ban6	zoeng6		keoi5	hai2	haak3	teng1	
high	*dye*	*bun*	*jerng*		*keoi*	*high*	*hahk*	*tang*	

Let's go play!

去 玩 啦 ！

heoi3 waan2 laa1

heoi wahn luh

扶手凳 Armchair
fu4 sau2 dang3 (*foo suw dung*)

窗口 Window
coeng1 hau2 (*cherng huw*)

花樽 Vase
faa1 zeon1 (*fah juun*)

畫 Painting
waa2 (*wah*)

檯 Table
toi2 (*toy*)

燈 Lamp
dang1 (*dung*)

波 Ball
bo1 (*buoh*)

地氈 Rug
dei6 zin1 (*day jeen*)

金魚 Goldfish
gam1 jyu4 (*gum yue*)

We **sing songs** together.

我	哋	一	齊	唱	歌	。
ngo5	dei6	jat1	cai4	coeng3	go1	
ngo	*day*	*yet*	*chai*	*cherng*	*guo*	

We play[*] piano together.

我 哋 一 齊 彈 鋼 琴 。

ngo5 dei6 jat1 cai4 taan4 gong3 kam4

ngo day yet chai tahn guong kum

[*] The translation of "play" varies based on context.

Who **wants** to go play in the **backyard**?

邊	個	想	去	後	院	玩	?
bin1	go3	soeng2	heoi3	hau6	jyun2	waan2	
bean	*guo*	*serng*	*heoi*	*huw*	*yuen*	*wahn*	

We like to **water** the **flowers**.

我	哋	鍾	意	淋	花	。
ngo5	dei6	zung1	ji3	lam4	faa1	
ngo	*day*	*johng*	*yee*	*lum*	*fa*	

花園 Flower Garden
faa1 jyun4 (*fa yuen*)

蝴蝶 Butterfly
wu4 dip2 (*woo deep*)

西瓜 Watermelon
sai1 gwaa1 (*sigh gwah*)

水喉 Garden Hose
seoi2 hau4 (*seoi huw*)

帽 Hat
mou2 (*moh*)

雀仔 Bird
zoek3 zai2 (*jerk zhai*)

草地 Lawn
cou2 dei6 (*cho day*)

雲 Cloud
wan4 (*wun*)

樹 Tree
syu6 (*shue*)

Everyone **climbs** the apple **trees**.

個 個 爬 蘋 果 樹 。

個	個	爬	蘋	果	樹
go3	go3	paa4	ping4	gwo2	syu6
guo	*guo*	*pah*	*ping*	*guo*	*shue*

Who wants to **pick** red apples?

邊	個	想	摘	紅	蘋	果	？
bin1	go3	soeng2	zaak6	hung4	ping4	gwo2	
bean	*guo*	*serng*	*jaak*	*hohng*	*ping*	*guo*	

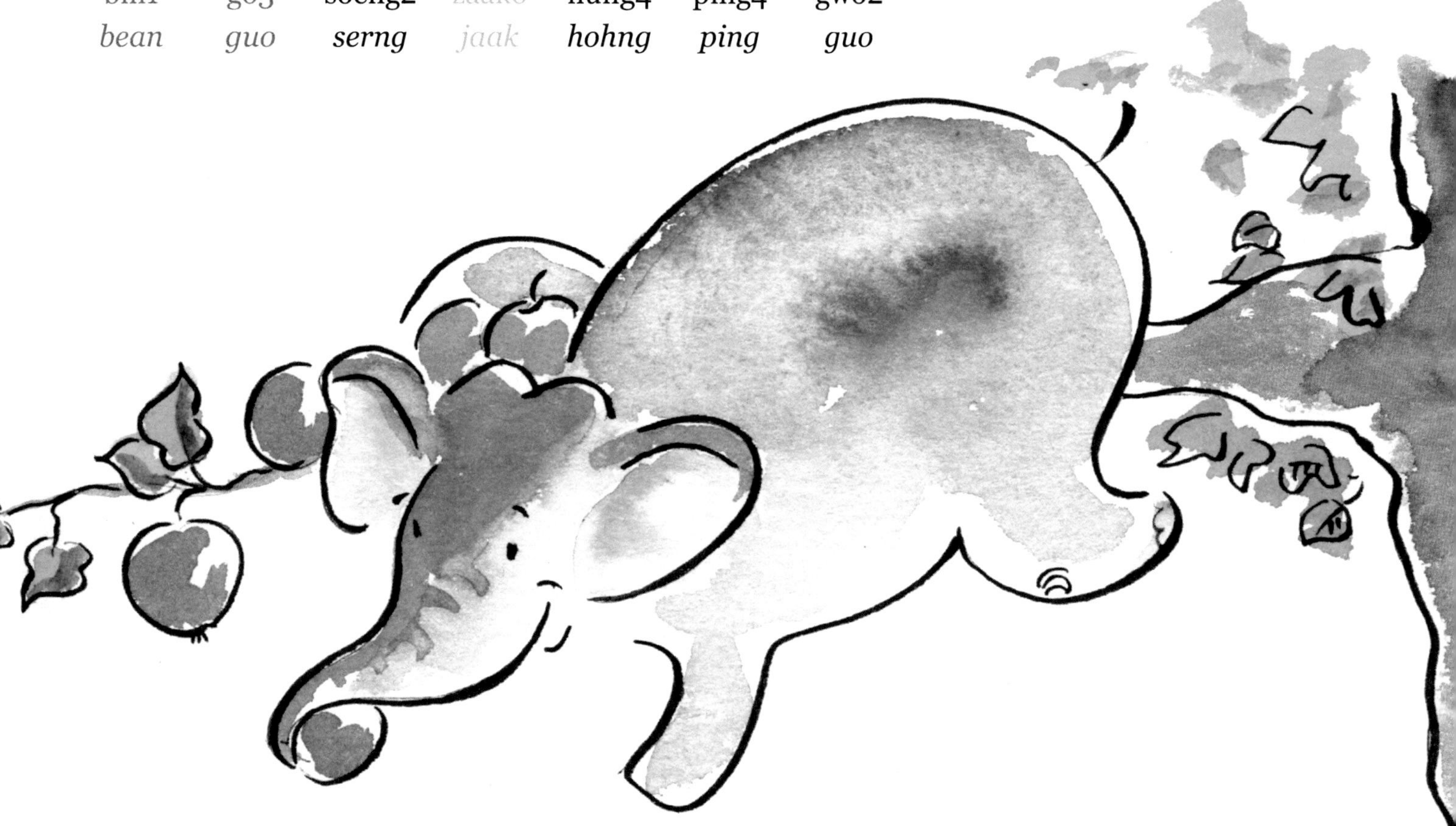

An **apple fell** down!

隻	蘋	果	跌	咗	落	地	喇	！
zek3	ping4	gwo2	dit3	zo2	lok6	dei6	laa3	
jaek	*ping*	*guo*	*deet*	*juo*	*lock*	*day*	*la*	

We like to play **ball**.

我	哋	鍾	意	打	波	。
ngo5	dei6	zung1	ji3	daa2	bo1	
ngo	*day*	*johng*	*yee*	*dah*	*buoh*	

We **fly** a **dragon kite**!

我	哋	放	條	龍	紙	鷂	！
ngo5	dei6	fong3	tiu4	lung4	zi2	jiu2	
ngo	*day*	*fuong*	*tiew*	*lohng*	*jee*	*yew*	

We played for so **long**! We're really **hungry**!

我	哋	玩	咗	好	耐	！	我	哋	好	肚	餓	！
ngo5	dei6	waan2	zo2	hou2	noi6		ngo5	dei6	hou2	tou5	ngo6	
ngo	*day*	*wahn*	*juo*	*ho*	*noy*		*ngo*	*day*	*ho*	*toe*	*ngoh*	

Everyone goes to the **kitchen**.

大 家 去 廚 房 。

daai6 gaa1 heoi3 cyu4 fong2

dye gah heoi chiu fuong

We help **cook dinner**!

我	哋	幫	手	煮	晚	飯	！
ngo5	dei6	bong1	sau2	zyu2	maan5	faan6	
ngo	*day*	*bong*	*suw*	*jue*	*mahn*	*fahn*	

凳 Chair
dang3 (*dung*)

碗 Bowl
wun2 (*woon*)

杯 Cup
bui1 (*buoy*)

鑊 Wok
wok6 (*wok*)

煲 Pot
bou1 (*bo*)

爐頭 Stove
lou4 tau4 (*lo tuw*)

焗爐 Oven
guk6 lou4 (*gook loh*)

雪櫃 Refrigerator
syut3 gwai6 (*shoot gwy*)

食飯檯 Dining Table
sik6 faan6 toi2 (*sik fahn toy*)

Tonight, we're eating noodle soup.
今 晚 食 湯 麵 。
gam1 maan5 sik6 tong1 min6
gum mahn sik tong mean

Who wants **boiled dumplings**?

邊	個	要	水	餃	？
bin1	go3	jiu3	seoi2	gaau2	
bean	*guo*	*yew*	*seoi*	*gao*	

魚 Fish
jyu4 (*yue*)

蛋 Egg
daan2 (*dahn*)

麵 Noodles
min6 (*mean*)

叉 Fork
caa1 (*cha*)

匙羹 Spoon
ci4 gang1 (*chee gung*)

筷子 Chopsticks
faai3 zi2 (fie jee)

牛奶 Milk
ngau4 naai5 (*nguw nigh*)

芥蘭 Chinese Broccoli
gaai3 laan2 (*guy lahn*)

紅蘿蔔 Carrot
hung4 lo4 baak6 (*huung luo bahk*)

After dinner, we go **take a bath**!

食	完	飯	，	我	哋	去	沖	涼	！
sik6	jyun4	faan6		ngo5	dei6	heoi3	cung1	loeng4	
sik	*yuen*	*fahn*		*ngo*	*day*	*heoi*	*chuong*	*lerng*	

We play with **soap bubbles**.

我 哋 玩 **番 梘 泡** 。

我	哋	玩	番	梘	泡
ngo5	dei6	waan2	faan1	gaan2	pou5
ngo	*day*	*wahn*	*fahn*	*gahn*	*poh*

水喉 Faucet
seoi2 hau4 (*seoi huw*)

牙刷 Toothbrush
ngaa4 caat2 (*nga chaht*)

牙膏 Toothpaste
ngaa4 gou1 (*nga go*)

沖涼巾 Bath Towel
cung1 loeng4 gan1 (*cho(ng) lerng gun*)

浴缸 Bathtub
juk6 gong1 (*yook guong*)

番梘 Soap
faan1 gaan2 (*fahn gahn*)

膠鴨仔 Toy Duck
gaau1 aap3 zai2 (*gau ahp zhai*)

鏡 Mirror
geng3 (*gang*)

瓷盆 Sink
ci4 pun2 (*chee poon*)

We **brush** our **teeth** and **wash** our **faces**.

我哋刷牙同埋洗面。

我	哋	刷	牙	同	埋	洗	面
ngo5	dei6	caat3	ngaa4	tung4	maai4	sai2	min6
ngo	*day*	*chaht*	*nga*	*tuong*	*my*	*sigh*	*mean*

Off to bed!

上 床 喇 !

soeng5 cong4 laa3

serng chong luh

⁺喇 is optional and adds emphasis.

In the **bedroom**, everyone **chooses** a book.

喺 睡 房 ， 每 人 揀 本 書 。

喺	睡	房	，	每	人	揀	本	書
hai2	seoi6	fong2		mui5	jan4	gaan2	bun2	syu1
high	*seoi*	*fuong*		*mui*	*yen*	*gahn*	*boon*	*shoe*

We **read books** together.

我	哋	一	齊	讀	書	。
ngo5	dei6	jat1	cai4	duk6	syu1	
ngo	*day*	*yet*	*chai*	*dook*	*shoe*	

書架 Bookshelf
syu1 gaa2 (*shoe gah*)

床 Bed
cong4 (*chong*)

被 Blanket
pei5 (*pay*)

枕頭 Pillow
zam2 tau4 (*jum tuw*)

書檯 Desk
syu1 toi2 (*shoe toy*)

奶樽 Milk Bottle
naai5 zeon1 (*nigh juun*)

恐龍 Dinosaur
hung2 lung4 (*hohng lohng*)

啤啤熊 Teddy Bear
be1 be1 hung4 (*beh beh hohng*)

月亮 Moon
jyut6 loeng6 (*yoot lerng*)

Time to **sleep**!

瞓 覺 喇！

fan3 gaau3 laa3

fun gau luh

Elephant helps us turn off the lights.

大	笨	象	幫	我	哋	熄	燈	。
daai6	ban6	zoeng6	bong1	ngo5	dei6	sik1	dang1	
dye	*bun*	*jerng*	*bong*	*ngo*	*day*	*sick*	*dung*	

Good night!

早唞！

zou2 tau2

jo tuw

NOTES

CANTONESE TONES Each Jyutping includes the tone (example: 貓 maau1 = tone 1). To remember the six tones in order, speak the numbers "394052"(saam1 gau2 sei3 ling4 ng5 ji6) in Cantonese.

TONE	NUMBER	JYUTPING	ALTERNATE PHONETICS
Tone 1	"3"	saam1	sahm
Tone 2	"9"	gau2	guw
Tone 3	"4"	sei3	say
Tone 4	"0"	ling4	ling
Tone 5	"5"	ng5	mm
Tone 6	"2"	ji6	yee

ALTERNATE PRONUNCIATIONS For words with more than one common pronunciation, this book tries to select the pronunciation that would be most easily understood when spoken by less fluent Cantonese speakers. For example, for 你(you): both "lei5 (lay)" and "nei5 (nay)" are common, but less fluent Cantonese speakers may find they are more easily understood when they speak "nei5 (nay)".

CLASSIFIERS Classifiers (or measure words) are used with nouns. Classifiers have similarities to English expressions such as a flock of geese, a piece of paper and a cup of water. These words are often optional in English, but are required in Cantonese. This book uses a few classifiers, including: 本 (bun2/boon) for furniture, 隻(zek3/jaek) for apple. If you are unsure which classifier to use, you can use the generic classifier 個 (go3/guo).

COLOR CODING

- Verbs (**CYAN** or **RED)**
- Nouns (**ORANGE** or **TEAL**)
- Other (**MAGENTA**)

ABOUT THE AUTHOR

K Yee is a Cantonese-American and native Cantonese speaker. She graduated from Stanford University and the Wharton School of Business, and was a National Spelling Bee finalist. She created Cantonese for Kids to help her own family have fun learning Cantonese.

ISBN: 9781955188067 (Hardcover); 9780999273067 (Paperback)
Green Cows Books: www.greencowsbooks.com

Made in the USA
Coppell, TX
12 August 2022